D0966786

Lao Tzu

TAO TE CHING

AN ILLUSTRATED

JOURNEY

Ex Libris

GIVEN TO

_____

BY

_____

ON

_____

LAO TZU

TAO TE CHING

AN ILLUSTRATED

JOURNEY

WATERCOLORS BY

Claudia Karabaic Sargent

EDITED BY PEG STREEP

FROM THE TRANSLATION BY JAMES LEGGE

A BULFINCH PRESS BOOK

LITTLE, BROWN AND COMPANY

Boston • New York • Toronto • London

For Frank and Felicity Rowfa, my life companions on The Way, with all my love

— C.K.S.

Compilation copyright © 1994 by Peg Streep
Illustrations copyright © 1994 by Claudia Karabaic Sargent

First Edition

Text design by Dede Cummings/IPA

Library of Congress Cataloging-in-Publication Data

Lao Tzu.
    [Tao te ching. English]
    Lao Tzu: Tao te ching : an illustrated journey / edited by Peg Streep from the translation by James Legge ; illustrated by Claudia Karabaic Sargent. — 1st ed.
      p.   cm.
    ISBN 0-8212-2075-6
    I. Streep, Peg. II. Legge, James, 1815–1897.
  III. Sargent, Claudia Karabaic. IV. Title.
  BL1900.L26E5   1993e
  299'.51482 — dc20   93-39655

Bulfinch Press is an imprint and trademark of Little, Brown and Company (Inc.)
Published simultaneously in Canada by Little, Brown & Company (Canada) Limited

PRINTED IN ITALY

Introduction

Since it was first introduced to the West in a Latin translation in the last decades of the eighteenth century, the *Tao Te Ching*, a sacred work both mystical and practical by turns, has captured the Western imagination. This little book of slightly more than five thousand Chinese characters — the whole of it shorter than the shortest of the Christian Gospels — continues to exert a profound influence; its paradoxes, its symbolism, its values, even the difficulty of its meaning, appear all the more vital as we approach the end of our century and the beginning of a new millennium.

The *Tao Te Ching* opens a door onto spiritual ways of thinking totally separate from those of the Western tradition. Its title, which may be literally translated as *The Book of the Way and Its Power*, sheds no light on its mysteries, since the Tao is no literal way or path or method. Indeed, in the opening lines we learn that even the word *Tao* is inadequate to encompass its meaning:

> The Tao that can be trodden is not the enduring and unchanging Tao.
> The name that can be named is not the enduring and unchanging name.

Modern scholarship has shown too that recourse to the work's history, its title, and even its author does little to clarify what remains shrouded in the work. Scholars, among them D. C. Lau and Robert Hendricks, now conjecture that the *Tao Te Ching*, once thought to have been written as early as the sixth century B.C., reflects the currents of thought of some three hundred years later, the late fourth or third centuries. Its title too, as we now know it, is a much later addition — first appearing in the second century A.D. — as is the traditional division of the book into two parts. Even the authorship of the *Tao Te Ching* is conjectural, although tradition, based on accounts dating from roughly 100 B.C., holds that it was written by a contemporary of Confucius (551–479 B.C.). The name Lao Tzu, though, which means "old philosopher" or "old person," suggests also that the "author" of the book of five thousand characters was not historical, but a personage meant to serve as an emblem of the philosophy and spirituality embodied in the work. D. C. Lau has even speculated that the *Tao Te Ching* (or *Lao Tzu*, as it is also called) is an anthology of spiritual sayings compiled by many hands.

For present-day readers, these mysteries may simply enhance the effect of reading the *Tao Te Ching*, its provocation of new thoughts and new ways of understanding which seem so separate from the world and society we live in. Effortless activity, after all, in the context of the *Tao Te Ching*, is not what we call "rolling off a log"; it is instead symbolized by water which, in its softness, seeks the lowest level, yet is strong enough to wear away the hardest substance. Even freedom in the *Tao Te Ching* takes on new meaning: it is freedom from desire, yet bound always by the true workings of the universe, the Tao itself.

This illustrated edition draws on images and symbols of Chinese art to express the mystery of the Tao; the text has been edited from the James Legge translation, first published in the waning years of the nineteenth century.

— P.S.

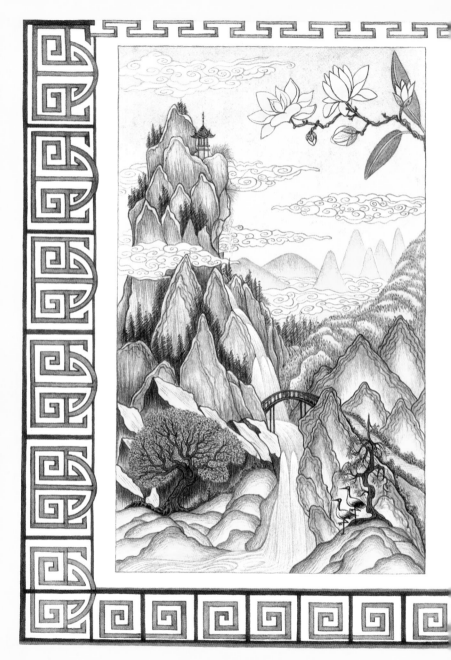

Part One

1

The Tao that can be trodden is not the enduring and unchanging Tao.

The name that can be named is not the enduring and unchanging name.

Having no name, it is the Originator of heaven and earth; having a name, it is the Mother of all things.

Without desire, we can plumb its depths; filled with desire, we can see only its externals.

Under these two aspects, it is really the same; but as it develops, it receives the different names.

Together we call them the Mystery; where the Mystery is deepest is the gate of all that is subtle and wonderful.

*A*ll in the world know the beauty of the beautiful, and in knowing they have knowledge of ugliness; they all know the skill of the skillful, and in knowing this they have knowledge of the unskilled.

So it is that that existence and nonexistence create each other;

So difficulty and ease produce each other;

So length and shortness fashion the one out of the figure of the other;

So height and lowness arise from the contrast of the one with the other;

So the musical notes and tones become harmonious through the relationship of one with another;

So before and after follow each other.

Therefore the sage acts without doing, and conveys his instructions without speech.

All things spring up, and there is not one which declines to show itself; they grow, and there is no claim made for their ownership; they go through their processes and there is no expectation of a reward at the end.

The work is accomplished without his laying claim to its merit.

Because the work is done without his laying claim to its merit, no one can take it away from him.

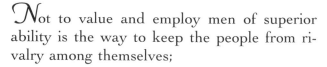

Not to value and employ men of superior ability is the way to keep the people from rivalry among themselves;

Not to prize hard-to-obtain articles is the way to keep them from becoming thieves;

Not to show them what is likely to excite their desires is the way to keep their minds from disorder.

Therefore the sage, in the exercise of his government, empties their minds, fills their bellies, weakens their will, and strengthens their bones.

He tries constantly to keep them without knowledge and without desire, and where there are those who have knowledge, to keep them from acting on it.

When there is this abstinence from action, good order is universal.

The Tao is the emptiness of a vessel and in our employment of it we must be on our guard against all fullness.

How deep and unfathomable it is, as if it were the source of all things!

We should blunt our sharp points, and unravel the complications of things; we should temper our brightness, and align ourselves with the obscurity of others.

How pure and eternally still the Tao is.

I do not know whose son it is. It might be older than God.

*H*eaven and earth do not act from any wish to be benevolent; they deal with all things as straw-dogs are dealt with.

The sages do not act from any wish to be benevolent; they deal with the people as straw-dogs are dealt with.

May not the space between heaven and earth be compared to a bellows? It is empty, yet powerful; moved again, it sends forth more air.

Talk leads only to fatigue; guard your inner being and keep it free.

The spirit of the Valley dies not.

It is the female mystery.

Its gate, from which they issued forth at first, is called the root from which grew heaven and earth.

Its power is enduring, used gently and without pain.

Heaven is long-enduring and earth continues long. The reason heaven and earth are able to endure and to continue is that they do not live of, or for, themselves. This is how they are able to continue and endure.

Therefore the sage puts his own person last, and yet it is found in the foremost place; he treats his person as if it were foreign to him, and yet that person is preserved.

Is it not because he has no personal and private ends that therefore such ends are realized?

The highest good is like that of water. The good of water appears in its benefiting all things, and in its occupying, without striving to leave, the low place which all men dislike. Hence its way is like that of the Tao.

The good of a home is in its location; the good of the mind is in its depths; the good of relationships in their virtuousness; the good of government in its securing order; the good of the conduct of affairs in its ability; the good of activity is in its timeliness.

And when a good man does not dispute his low position, no one finds fault with him.

It is better to leave a vessel unfilled than to try to carry it when it is full.

If you keep feeling a point that has been sharpened, the point cannot long preserve its sharpness.

When gold and jade fill the hall, their owner cannot keep them safe.

When wealth and honors lead to arrogance, this brings its evil on itself.

When the work is done, and one's name is becoming distinguished, to withdraw into obscurity is the way of Heaven.

When the intelligent and animal souls are united in one embrace, they can be kept from separating.

When he gives undivided attention to the vital breath and brings it to the utmost degree of pliancy, he can become as a newborn.

When he has cleansed the most mysterious sights of his imagination, he can become flawless.

In loving the people and ruling the state, cannot he proceed without any purpose of act? In the opening and shutting of his gates of heaven, cannot he do so as a female bird? While his intelligence reaches in every direction, cannot he appear to be without knowledge?

The Tao produces all things and nourishes them;

It produces them and does not claim them as its own;

It does all, and yet does not boast of it;

It presides over all, and yet does not control them.

This is what is called The Mysterious Quality of the Tao.

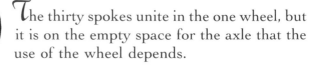

The thirty spokes unite in the one wheel, but it is on the empty space for the axle that the use of the wheel depends.

Clay is fashioned into vessels, but it is on their hollow emptiness that their use depends.

The door and windows are cut from the walls to form a room, but it is on the empty space within that its use depends.

Therefore, what has positive existence serves for profitable adaptation, and what has not, for actual usefulness.

The five hues of color blind the eyes;
    The five notes of ·music deafen the ears;
    The five flavors deprive the mouth of taste;
    The chariot course and hunting make the
mind mad;
    Coveting rarities changes man's conduct
to evil.

Therefore the sage seeks to satisfy the
craving of the belly and not that of the eyes.
He puts from him the latter, and prefers to
seek the former.

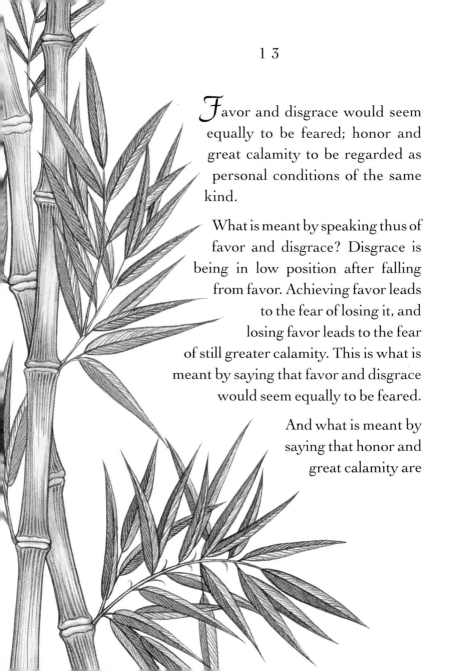

13

*F*avor and disgrace would seem equally to be feared; honor and great calamity to be regarded as personal conditions of the same kind.

What is meant by speaking thus of favor and disgrace? Disgrace is being in low position after falling from favor. Achieving favor leads to the fear of losing it, and losing favor leads to the fear of still greater calamity. This is what is meant by saying that favor and disgrace would seem equally to be feared.

And what is meant by saying that honor and great calamity are

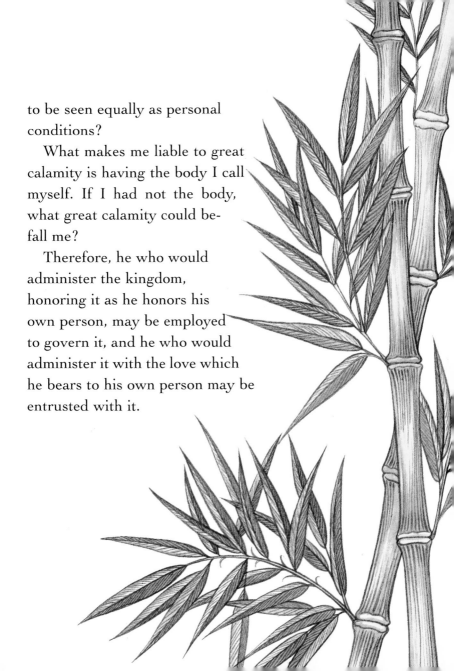

to be seen equally as personal conditions?

What makes me liable to great calamity is having the body I call myself. If I had not the body, what great calamity could befall me?

Therefore, he who would administer the kingdom, honoring it as he honors his own person, may be employed to govern it, and he who would administer it with the love which he bears to his own person may be entrusted with it.

e look at it, and we do not see it, and we name it The Unvarying.

We listen to it, and we do not hear it, and we name it The Inaudible.

We try to grasp it, and we cannot get hold of it, and we name it The Subtle.

With these three qualities, it cannot be made the subject of description, and hence we blend them together to obtain The One.

Its upper part is not bright, and its lower part is not obscure.

Ceaseless in its action, it yet cannot be named,
and then it again returns and becomes nothing.

This is called the Form of the Formless,
and the Semblance of the Invisible; this is
called the Fleeting and Indeterminable.

We meet it and do not see its front;
we follow it and do not see its back.

When we can lay hold of the Tao of old
to direct the things of the present,
and are able to know it as it was of
old in the beginning, this is
called the unwinding of the
thread of the Tao.

The old skillful masters of the Tao comprehended its mysteries with subtle and exquisite penetration, and were profound so as to elude men's knowledge. As they were thus beyond men's knowledge, I will try to describe what they appeared to be.

They looked timid like those who wade through a stream in winter; irresolute like those who are afraid of all around them; grave like a guest in awe of his host; evanescent like ice that is melting away; unpretentious like wood that has not been fashioned into anything; vacant like a valley; dull like muddied waters.

Who can make the muddy water clear? Let it be still, and it will gradually become clear.

Who can secure the condition of rest? Let movement go on, and the condition of rest will gradually take place.

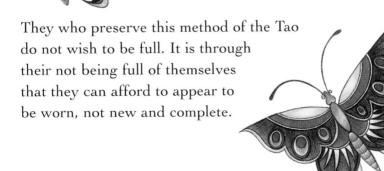

They who preserve this method of the Tao do not wish to be full. It is through their not being full of themselves that they can afford to appear to be worn, not new and complete.

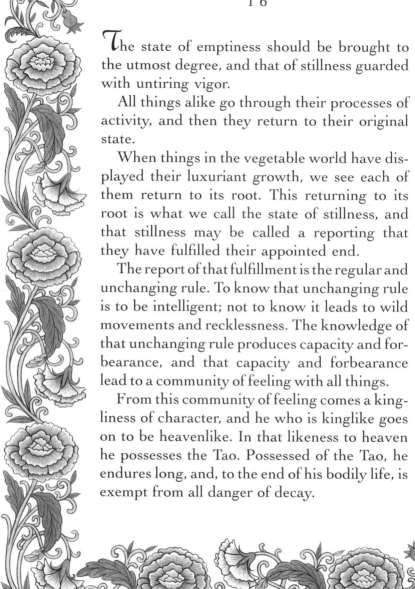

The state of emptiness should be brought to the utmost degree, and that of stillness guarded with untiring vigor.

All things alike go through their processes of activity, and then they return to their original state.

When things in the vegetable world have displayed their luxuriant growth, we see each of them return to its root. This returning to its root is what we call the state of stillness, and that stillness may be called a reporting that they have fulfilled their appointed end.

The report of that fulfillment is the regular and unchanging rule. To know that unchanging rule is to be intelligent; not to know it leads to wild movements and recklessness. The knowledge of that unchanging rule produces capacity and forbearance, and that capacity and forbearance lead to a community of feeling with all things.

From this community of feeling comes a kingliness of character, and he who is kinglike goes on to be heavenlike. In that likeness to heaven he possesses the Tao. Possessed of the Tao, he endures long, and, to the end of his bodily life, is exempt from all danger of decay.

*I*n the earliest times, the people did not know their rulers existed.

In the next age, they loved them and praised them.

In the next they feared them.

In the next they despised them.

Thus it was that when the faith in the Tao was deficient in the rulers, a want of faith in the rulers ensued in the people.

How irresolute did those earliest rulers appear in their reticence in speaking, refusing their words importance? Their work was done and their undertakings were successful, while the people all said, "We are as we are, of ourselves!"

When the great Tao ceased to be observed, benevolence and righteousness came into vogue. Then appeared wisdom and shrewdness, and there ensued great hypocrisy.

When harmony no longer prevailed throughout the six kinships, sons found their filial duty; when the states and clans fell into disorder, loyal ministers appeared.

*I*f we could renounce our sagacity and discard our wisdom, it would be better for the
people a hundredfold.

If we could renounce our benevolence and
discard our righteousness, the people
would again become filial and kindly.

If we could renounce our artful contrivances and discard our scheming for gain,
there would be no thieves or robbers.

Those three methods of governing
thought the old ways lacking in ele-
gance, and set forth these names to
veil their worthlessness. The plain
course and the simple view
eschew selfish ends
and lusts.

When we renounce learning, we are without trouble.

How to distinguish the "Yes" which is readiness, and the "Yes" which is flattery when little difference is displayed?

What fills the gulf between Good and Evil?

What all men fear is indeed to be feared, but how wide and without end is the range of questions asking to be answered.

The multitude of men look satisfied and pleased, as if enjoying a full banquet, or enjoying the view from a tower in spring.

I alone seem listless and still, my desires having as yet given no sign of their presence.

I am like an infant who has not yet smiled. I look dejected and forlorn, as if I had no home to go to.

The multitude of men all have enough and to spare.

I alone seem to have lost everything. My mind is that of a stupid man. I am in a state of chaos.

Ordinary men look bright and intelligent, while I alone seem to be benighted.

They look full of discrimination, while I alone am witless and confused. I seem to be carried about as if on the sea, drifting as if I had nowhere to rest.

All men have their spheres of action, while I alone seem dull and incapable, like a crude outsider.

Thus I alone am different from other men, but I seek the sustenance of the Mother.

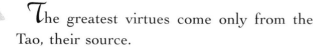

The greatest virtues come only from the Tao, their source.

Who can tell the nature of the Tao? It flies out of our sight and eludes our touch.

The forms of all things crouch within it,
Eluding touch and sight;

Only the semblance of all things remains.
The Tao is profound, dark and obscure;
The essence of all things endures there.

Those essences enfold the truth,
Yielding all that, when seen,
can be told.

It is so now. It was always so.
Its name is the eternal essence;

Thus all things form without end.

How do I know that it is so with all the beauties of existing things? By this, the nature of the Tao.

The partial becomes complete;

The crooked becomes straight;

The empty becomes full;

The worn out becomes new.

He whose desires are few fulfills them; he whose desires are many goes astray.

Therefore the sage holds in his embrace the one thing and manifests it to all the world.

He is free from self-display, and therefore he shines;

He is free from self-assertion and therefore he is distinguished;

He is free from self-boasting, and therefore his merit is acknowledged;

He is free from self-complacency, and therefore he acquires superiority.

Because he is thus free from striving, therefore no one in the world is able to strive against him.

The saying of the ancients that "the partial becomes complete" was not vainly spoken. All real completion is comprehended under it.

*A*bstaining from speech marks him who obeys the spontaneity of his nature. A violent wind does not last for a whole morning; a sudden rain does not last for the whole day. For these things, Heaven and Earth are responsible, and if Heaven and Earth cannot extend these actions, how much less can man?

Therefore, when one follows the Tao, those who also pursue it agree with him in it, and those who set their sights on the manifestations of its course agree with him in that, while even those who fail in the study and practice of the Tao agree with him while they fail.

Hence those with whom he agrees as to the Tao have the happiness of attaining it; those with whom he agrees as to its manifestation have the happiness of attaining it; and those with whom he agrees in their failure have also the happiness of attaining to the Tao.

But where his faith is insufficient, a want of faith in him ensues on the part of the others.

$\mathcal{H}$e who walks on his tiptoes does not stand steady; he who strides, walks unevenly.

He who displays himself does not shine; he who asserts his own views is not distinguished.

He who vaunts himself does not find his merit acknowledged; he who is self-conceited has no superiority allowed to him.

From the standpoint of the Tao, these are like leftover crumbs of food, or extraneous growths. Hence those who pursue the course of the Tao do not allow them.

$\mathcal{T}$here was something undefined, and yet complete, coming into existence before Heaven and Earth.

How still it was and formless, standing alone, and undergoing no change, reaching everywhere and in no danger of being exhausted.

It may be regarded as the Mother of all things.

I do not know its name, and I give it the designation of the Tao.

Trying to name it further, I call it The Great.

Being great, it flows constantly. Flowing, it becomes remote. Having become remote, it returns. Therefore the Tao is great; Heaven is great; Earth is great; and the King is also great. In the universe there are four that are great, and the King is one of them.

Man takes his law from the Earth; the Earth takes its law from Heaven; Heaven takes its law from the Tao. The law of the Tao is its being what it is.

Gravity is the root of lightness; stillness is the ruler of movement.

Therefore the sage, marching the day long, does not go far from his baggage wagons. Although he may have brilliant prospects to observe, he remains quietly indifferent to them.

How should the lord of a myriad chariots carry himself lightly before the kingdom? If he acts lightly, he has lost his root of gravity; if he proceeds to active movement, he will lose his throne.

The skilled traveler leaves no tracks from his wheels nor traces of his footsteps; the skilled speaker says nothing that can be found fault with or blamed; the skilled calculator needs no columns; he who closes skillfully needs no bolts or bars, while to open what he has shut will be impossible; the skilled binder uses no strings or knots, while to unloose what he has bound will be impossible.

In the same way the sage is always skilled at saving men, and so he does not cast away any man; he is always skilled at saving things and so he does not cast away anything. This is to be called "Hiding the light of his procedure."

Therefore the man of skill is a master to be looked up to by him who is unskilled; and he who is unskilled is the helper of he who has the skills. If the one did not honor his master and the other did not rejoice in his helper, an observer, though intelligent, might greatly err about them. This is called "The utmost degree of mystery."

Who knows the masculine,
Yet maintains the feminine;
As many streams flow into one channel,
All come to him beneath the sky.

Thus he retains the constant excellence,
And becomes the stainless, simple child
again.

Who knows the attraction of white,
But keeps himself in the shade of black,
Displays the pattern of humility
In the view of all beneath the sky.

He is arrayed in unchanging excellence,
He returns to man's first limitless state.

He who knows how glory
shines,
    Yet loves disgrace and is
not paled by it,
    He becomes like a spacious
valley
    To which all men come from beneath
the sky.

    The unchanging excellence is complete:
    We hail the simple infant in the man.

Divided and distributed, the unworked mate-
rial yields vessels. The sage, when employed,
becomes the ruler, and in his rule employs no
violent measures.

𝒥f anyone should wish to acquire the kingdom for himself, and to effect this by doing, I see that he will not succeed.

The kingdom is a spiritlike thing and cannot be gotten by active doing. He who would so win it, destroys it; he who would so hold it in his grasp, loses it.

The course and nature of things is such: what was once front is now behind; what was first warmed is now freezing; what was once weakness is now strength; what was once built is now ruined.

Hence the sage renounces excessive effort, extravagance, and easy indulgence.

$\mathcal{H}$e who would assist a lord of men in harmony with the Tao will not assert his mastery in the kingdom by force of arms. Such a course will only re-bound upon itself.

Wherever an army is stationed, briars and thorns spring up. In the sequence of great armies there are sure to be bad years.

A skilled commander strikes a decisive blow, and stops. He does not dare to assert and complete his mastery. He will strike the blow, but will be on his guard against being vain or boastful or arrogant. He strikes the blow as a matter of necessity; he strikes it without a need for mastery.

When things have attained their maturity, they become old. This may be said not to be in accordance with the Tao, and what is not in accordance with it soon comes to an end.

$\mathcal{N}$ow weapons, however beautiful, are instruments of evil omen, hateful to all creatures. Therefore they who have the Tao do not like to employ them.

The superior man ordinarily considers the left hand the most honorable place, but, in time of war, it is the right hand.

Those sharp weapons are instruments of evil omen, and not the instruments of the superior man; he uses them only on the compulsion of necessity.

Calm and repose are what he prizes; victory by force of arms is undesirable to him. To consider victory desirable would be to delight in the slaughter of men; and he who delights in the slaughter of men cannot get his will in the kingdom.

On occasions of festivity, the prized position is that of the left hand; on occasions of mourning, the right hand. The second in command of the army has his place on the left; the commander in chief has his place on the right, the place assigned to him by the rites of mourning.

He who has killed multitudes of men should weep for them with the bitterest of grief, and the victor in battle has his place according to those rites.

The Tao, considered as unchanging, has no name.

Though in its primordial simplicity it may be small, the whole world does not presume to demean it. If a prince or king could guard and hold it, all would spontaneously submit themselves to him.

Under the Tao's guidance, Heaven and Earth unite together and send down the sweet dew which, without the directions of men, reaches equally everywhere of its own accord.

As soon as it proceeds to action, it has a name. Once it has that name, men can know to rest in it. When they know to rest in it, they can be free from all risk and failure.

The relation of the Tao to all the world is like that of the great rivers and seas to the streams from the valleys.

He who knows other men is discerning; he who knows himself is intelligent.

He who overcomes others is strong; he who overcomes himself is mighty.

He who is satisfied with his lot is rich; he who goes on acting with energy has a will.

He who does not fail in the requirements of his position continues long; he who dies and yet does not perish has longevity.

*A*ll-pervading is the Great Tao! It may be found on the left hand and on the right.

All things depend on it for their production, which it gives to them; not one refuses obedience to it. When its work is accomplished, it does not claim the name of accomplishment. It clothes all things as if with a garment, and makes no assumption of being their lord; it may be named in the smallest things.

All things return, and do not know that it is the Tao that presides over their returning; it may be named in the greatest things.

Hence the sage is able, in the same way, to accomplish his great achievements. It is by not making himself great that he can accomplish great things.

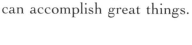

To him who holds in his hands the great image, the whole world repairs. Men resort to him and receive no hurt but find rest, peace, and feeling of ease.

Music and sweets will make the passing guest repair. But though the Tao seems insipid and has no flavor, though it seems not worth looking at or being listened to, the use of it is inexhaustible.

When he is about to inhale, he must first exhale;

When he weakens another, he will first strengthen him;

When he strives to overthrow, he must first raise up;

When he will plunder another, he must first make gifts to him.

This is called "Hiding the light."

The soft overcomes the hard, and the weak the strong.
Fish should not be taken from the deep; instruments for the profit of a state should not be shown to the people.

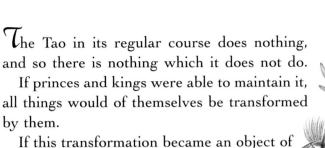

The Tao in its regular course does nothing, and so there is nothing which it does not do.

If princes and kings were able to maintain it, all things would of themselves be transformed by them.

If this transformation became an object of my desire, I would express the desire by the nameless simplicity.

The nameless simplicity is free from all external aim, desireless, at rest and still; all things go right as of their own accord.

Part Two

3 8

Those who possessed the attributes in the highest degree did not show them, and therefore they possessed them in fullest measure. Those who possessed those attributes in a lower degree sought not to lose them, and therefore they did not possess them in fullest measure.

Those who possessed those attributes in the highest degree did nothing, and had no need to do anything. Those who possessed them in a lower degree were doing, and had need to be so doing.

Those who possessed the highest benevolence were always seeking to carry it out, and had no need to. Those who possessed the highest righteousness were always seeking to carry it out, and had need to be so doing.

Those who possessed the highest propriety sought to show it, and when men did not respond to it, they rolled up their sleeves and asserted it by force.

Thus it was that when the Tao was lost, its attributes appeared; when its attributes were lost, benevolence appeared; when benevolence was lost, righteousness appeared; and when righteousness was lost, the proprieties appeared.

Propriety is the attenuated form of true-heartedness and good faith, and is also the commencement of disorder; swift apprehension is only a flower of the Tao, and is the beginning of stupidity.

Thus it is that the Great Man abides by what is solid, and avoids what is flimsy, and dwells with the fruit and not with the flower. It is thus that he puts away the one and makes choice of the other.

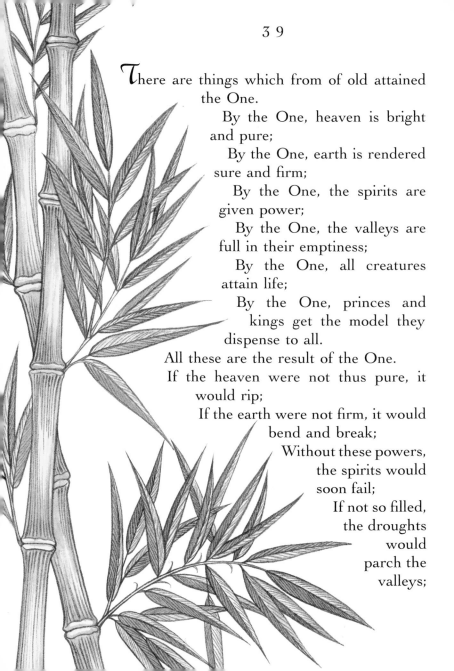

There are things which from of old attained the One.

By the One, heaven is bright and pure;

By the One, earth is rendered sure and firm;

By the One, the spirits are given power;

By the One, the valleys are full in their emptiness;

By the One, all creatures attain life;

By the One, princes and kings get the model they dispense to all.

All these are the result of the One.

If the heaven were not thus pure, it would rip;

If the earth were not firm, it would bend and break;

Without these powers, the spirits would soon fail;

If not so filled, the droughts would parch the valleys;

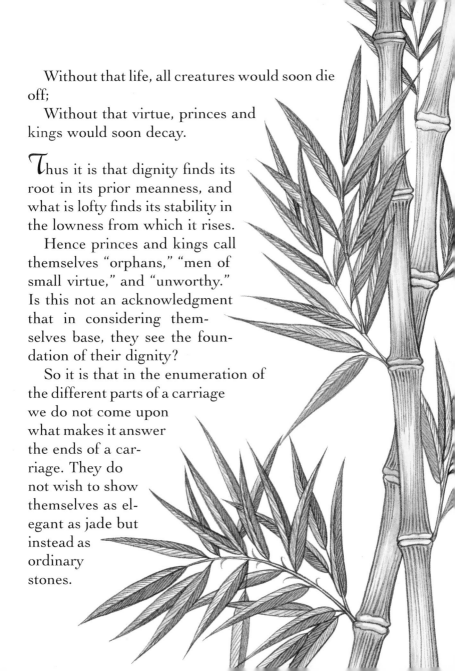

Without that life, all creatures would soon die off;

Without that virtue, princes and kings would soon decay.

Thus it is that dignity finds its root in its prior meanness, and what is lofty finds its stability in the lowness from which it rises.

Hence princes and kings call themselves "orphans," "men of small virtue," and "unworthy." Is this not an acknowledgment that in considering themselves base, they see the foundation of their dignity?

So it is that in the enumeration of the different parts of a carriage we do not come upon what makes it answer the ends of a carriage. They do not wish to show themselves as elegant as jade but instead as ordinary stones.

The movement of the Tao proceeds by contraries, and weakness marks the course of Tao's mighty deeds.

All things under heaven sprang from It as existing and named; that existence sprang from It as nonexistent and unnamed.

When the wisest scholars hear about the Tao, they put it into practice. When mediocre scholars hear about the Tao, they seem now to keep and now to lose it. When worthless scholars hear about the Tao, they laugh at it uproariously. If it were not laughed at, it would not be fit to be the Tao.

Therefore the sages have thus expressed themselves:

The Tao, when it is brightest, appears to lack light;

To progress in it, is to appear to lose ground;
Its even way is rocky and jagged;
Its highest virtue rises from the depths;
Its greatest beauty appears to offend the eyes;
And he who has most owns least.
Its solid truth seems ever-changing;
Its largest square is cornerless;
Its great vessel is slow in the making;
Its sound is loud, but it is wordless;
A semblance great, the shadow of a shade.

The Tao is hidden, and has no name; but it is the Tao which imparts to all things what they need, and makes them complete.

The Tao produced One; One produced Two; Two produced Three; Three produced All Things.

All things leave behind them the Obscurity out of which they have come, and go forward to embrace the Light into which they have emerged, while they are harmonized by the Breath of Vacancy.

What men dislike is to be orphans, to have little virtue, to be unworthy; yet these are the designations which princes and kings use for themselves. So it is that some things are increased by being diminished, and others are diminished by being increased.

What other men teach, I also teach. The violent and strong do not die their natural deaths. I will make this the basis of my teaching.

The softest thing in the world dashes against and overcomes the hardest; that which has no substantial existence enters where there is no crevice. I know thereby what advantage belongs to doing nothing.

There are few in the world who attain to the teaching without words and the advantage arising from nonaction.

Which is more important: fame or life?

Which is more valuable: life or wealth?

Keep life and lose those other things; keep them, and lose your life. Which brings more sorrow?

Thus we may see that he who holds to fame rejects what is greater; he who loves his goods gives up true riches.

He who is content need not fear disgrace; he who knows how to stop incurs no blame and shall live long free from danger.

Great achievements seem lacking,

But their vigor enduring;

Great fullness seems empty,

But its use is exhaustible;

The straight is deemed crooked,

The most skilled deemed crude,

The most eloquent seems a stammering scream.

Constant action overcomes cold; being still overcomes heat. Purity and stillness give the correct law to all under heaven.

When the Tao prevails in the world, they send back their swift horses to draw the dung carts. When the Tao is disregarded in the world, the war-horses breed in the borderlands.

There is no guilt greater than to sanction ambition; no calamity greater than to be discontented with one's lot; no fault greater than the wish to acquire. Therefore the sufficiency of contentment is an enduring and unchanging sufficiency.

Without leaving his house, he understands all that takes place under the sky; without looking outside his window, he sees the Tao of Heaven. The farther he goes out from himself, the less he knows.

Therefore the sages knew without traveling; gave names to things without seeing them; and accomplished their ends without any purpose of doing so.

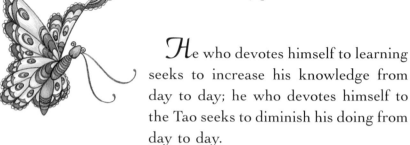

$\mathcal{H}$e who devotes himself to learning seeks to increase his knowledge from day to day; he who devotes himself to the Tao seeks to diminish his doing from day to day.

He diminishes it and diminishes it again until purposefully he achieves doing nothing. Achieving non-action, there is nothing which he does not do.

He who gets all under heaven as his own does so by not troubling himself with that end. He who troubles himself with that end is not equal to getting all under heaven.

The sage has no invariable mind of his own; he makes the mind of the people his mind.

To those who are good, I am good; and to those who are not good, I am also good, and thus get to be good. To those who are sincere, I am sincere; and to those who are not sincere, I am also sincere, and thus get to be sincere.

In the world, the sage has the appearance of indecision and keeps his mind in a state of indifference to all. The people all keep their eyes and ears directed to him, and he deals with them all as his children.

*M*en come forth and live; they enter and die. Of every ten, three are ministers of life and three are ministers of death.

There are also three in every ten whose aim is to live, but whose movements tend to the land of death. And for what reason? Because of their excessive endeavors to perpetuate life.

But I have heard that he who is skillful in managing the life entrusted to him travels on the land without having to shun rhinoceros or tiger, and goes into battle without armor or sharp weapon. The rhinoceros finds no place to thrust its horn, nor the tiger a place to fix its claws, nor the weapon a place to admit its point. And for what reason? Because, in him, there is no place of death.

*A*ll things are produced by the Tao and nourished by its outflowing operation. They receive their forms according to the nature of each, and are completed according to the circumstances of their condition. Therefore all things without exception honor the Tao, and exalt its outflowing operation.

This honoring of the Tao and exalting of its operation is not the result of any ordination but is always a spontaneous tribute.

Thus it is that the Tao produces all things, nourishes them, brings them to their full growth, nurses them, completes them, matures them, maintains them, and shelters them.

It produces them and makes no claim to the possession of them; it carries them through their processes and does not vaunt its ability in doing so; it brings them to maturity and exercises no control over them. This is called its mysterious operation.

The Tao which originated all under the sky is to be considered the mother of them all.

When the mother is found, we know what her children should be.

When one knows that he is his mother's child and proceeds to guard the mother within him, he will be free from peril to the end of his life.

Let him keep his mouth and his nostrils closed, and all of his life he will be free from laborious exertion. Let him keep his mouth open and expend his breath in the promotion of his acts, and all of his life there will be no safety for him.

The perception of what is small is clear-sightedness; the guarding of what is soft and tender is strength.

He who uses his light well, reverting to its bright source, will stay safe, and hides the unchanging from the sight of men.

*I*f I were suddenly to become known and able to act according to the great Tao, what I should be most afraid of would be a boastful display.

The great Tao is very level and easy, but people love the byways.

Their courts shall be well kept, but their fields shall be badly cultivated, and their granaries very empty. They shall wear elegant and ornamented robes, carry the sharpest of swords, pamper themselves in eating and drinking, and have a super-abundance of property and wealth. Such princes may be called robbers and boasters. Surely this is contrary to the Tao.

What the skillful planter plants can never be uprooted; What his skillful arms enfold cannot be taken from him. Sons shall bring sacrifices to his shrine for generations.

When nursed within the self, Tao makes virtue true. In the family where Tao rules, virtue will grow. In the neighborhood where Tao prevails, virtue will abound. In the state where Tao pervades, virtue will thrive. Employ it throughout the kingdom and virtue will will flourish.

In this way, the effect will be seen in the person, in the family, in the neighborhood, and in the kingdom.

How do I know this effect is sure to hold thus all under the sky? By this method of observation.

He who has the attributes of the Tao abundantly in himself is like an infant. Poisonous insects will not sting him; fierce beasts will not seize him; birds of prey will not strike him.

The infant's bones are weak and its sinews are soft, yet its grasp is firm. It does not yet know the union of male and female, yet its virile member may still be excited, showing the perfection of its physical essence. All day long it will cry without hoarseness, showing the harmony of its constitution.

Thus the unchanging Tao is shown to him who knows this harmony, and in the knowledge is wisdom. All life-increasing arts turn to evil; where the mind incites the vital breath, the strength is false.

When things have become strong, they become old, which may be said to be contrary to the Tao. Whatever is contrary to the Tao soon ends.

He who knows the Tao does not speak; he who is ever ready to speak about it, does not know it.

He who knows it will close his mouth and his nostrils. He will blunt his sharp points and unravel the complications of things; he will shade his brightness and bring himself into agreement with obscurity. This is called The Mysterious Agreement.

He cannot be treated familiarly or distantly; he is beyond all consideration of profit or injury, of nobility or baseness.

He is the noblest man under Heaven.

$\mathcal{A}$ state may be ruled by correction, and weapons of war may be used with crafty dexterity, but the kingdom is made one's own only by freedom from action and purpose.

How do I know that this is so? By these facts: multiple taboos increase the poverty of the people; the more sharp tools the people have to add to their profit, the greater disorder in the state and clan; the more acts of crafty dexterity, the more strange contrivances appear; the more display there is of laws and edicts, the greater the number of thieves and robbers.

Therefore, a sage has said, "I will do nothing, and the people will be transformed of themselves; I will keep still, and the people will of themselves become correct. I will take no trouble, and the people will of themselves become rich; I will manifest no ambition, and the people will of themselves attain to the primitive simplicity."

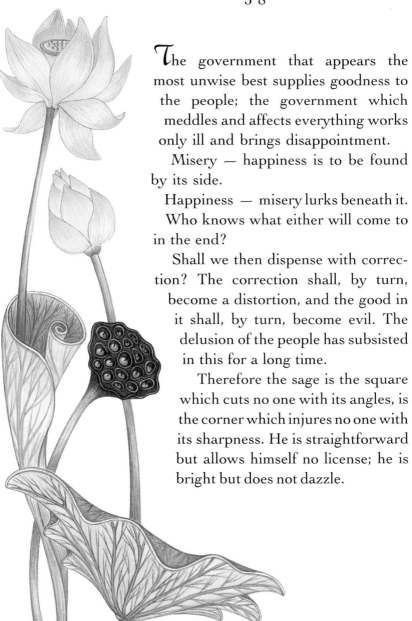

The government that appears the most unwise best supplies goodness to the people; the government which meddles and affects everything works only ill and brings disappointment.

Misery — happiness is to be found by its side.

Happiness — misery lurks beneath it. Who knows what either will come to in the end?

Shall we then dispense with correction? The correction shall, by turn, become a distortion, and the good in it shall, by turn, become evil. The delusion of the people has subsisted in this for a long time.

Therefore the sage is the square which cuts no one with its angles, is the corner which injures no one with its sharpness. He is straightforward but allows himself no license; he is bright but does not dazzle.

In governing men and in serving Heaven, there is nothing like moderation.

This moderation effects an early return to virtue. That early return is what I call the repeated accumulation of virtue. With that repeated accumulation of virtue, there comes the subjugation of every obstacle to the return of virtue. Of this subjugation we know not what shall be the limit; and one who knows not what the limit shall be, he may be the ruler of the state.

He who possesses the mother of the state may continue long. His case is like that of the plant, of which we say that its roots are deep and its flower stalk firm.

This is the way to secure that its enduring life shall long be seen.

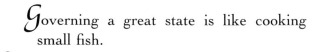

*G*overning a great state is like cooking small fish.

Let the kingdom be governed according to the Tao, and the spirits of the dead will not manifest their spiritual energy. It is not that those spirits have no spiritual energy, but it will not be employed to hurt men. It is not that it could not hurt men, but neither does the ruling sage hurt them.

When these two do not affect each other with injury, their good influences converge in the virtue of the Tao.

What makes a great state is its being a low-lying, down-flowing stream. It becomes the feminine center toward which all flow under heaven.

The female always overcomes the male by her stillness, by lowering herself through her stillness.

Thus it is that a great state, by lowering itself to small states, gains them for itself; and that small states, by lowering themselves to a great state, win it over to them. In the one case the lowering leads to gaining adherents, in the other case to procuring favor.

The great state only wishes to unite men together and nourish them; a small state only wishes to be received by, and to serve, the other.

Each gets what it desires, but the great state must learn to lower itself.

Of all things, Tao has the most honored place. It is good men's richest treasure; it guards bad men and effaces their evil.

Its admirable words can purchase honor; its admirable deeds can raise their performer above others. Even men who are not good are not abandoned by it.

Therefore when the sovereign occupies his place as the Son of Heaven and has appointed his three ducal ministers, even though a prince were to send in a symbol of rank so large as to fill both hands and a fine team of horses, such an offering would not be equal to this Tao, which he might present on his knees.

Why was it that the ancients prized this Tao so much? Was it not because it could be gotten by seeking for it, and the guilty could escape by it? This is the reason why all under heaven consider it the most valuable thing.

To act without acting; to conduct affairs without effort; to taste without discerning any flavor; to consider what is small great and a few as many; and to recompense injury with kindness.

The master of the Tao anticipates things that are difficult while they are easy, and does things that would become great when they are small.

All difficult things in the world arise from a previous state in which they were easy, and all great things from a state in which they were small.

Therefore the sage, while he never does what is great, is able to accomplish the greatest things.

He who promises lightly is sure to keep but little faith; he who continually thinks things easy is sure to find them difficult.

Therefore the sage sees difficulty even in what seems easy, and so never has any difficulties.

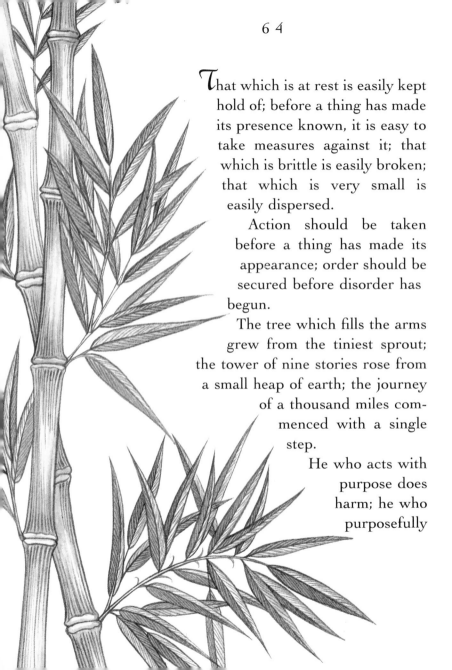

That which is at rest is easily kept hold of; before a thing has made its presence known, it is easy to take measures against it; that which is brittle is easily broken; that which is very small is easily dispersed.

Action should be taken before a thing has made its appearance; order should be secured before disorder has begun.

The tree which fills the arms grew from the tiniest sprout; the tower of nine stories rose from a small heap of earth; the journey of a thousand miles commenced with a single step.

He who acts with purpose does harm; he who purposefully

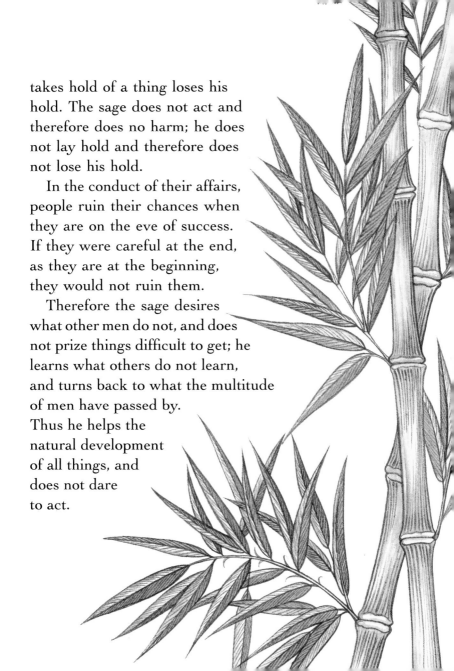

takes hold of a thing loses his hold. The sage does not act and therefore does no harm; he does not lay hold and therefore does not lose his hold.

In the conduct of their affairs, people ruin their chances when they are on the eve of success. If they were careful at the end, as they are at the beginning, they would not ruin them.

Therefore the sage desires what other men do not, and does not prize things difficult to get; he learns what others do not learn, and turns back to what the multitude of men have passed by. Thus he helps the natural development of all things, and does not dare to act.

The ancients who showed their skill in practicing the Tao did so not to enlighten the people but rather to make them simple and ignorant.

The difficulty in governing the people arises from their having too much knowledge. He who governs a state by his wisdom is a scourge to it, while he who does not is a blessing.

He who knows these two things finds in them also his model and rule. The ability to know this model and rule constitutes what we call the mysterious excellence.

Deep and far-reaching is such mysterious excellence, showing its possessor as opposite to others but leading them to a great conformity to him.

What allows the rivers and seas to receive the homage and tribute of all the valley streams is that they are low-lying; it is thus that they are the kings of them all. So it is that the sage, wishing to be above men, places himself below them with his words and, wishing to be before them, places his person behind them.

In this way, though he has his place above them, men do not feel his weight nor, though he has his place before them, do they feel it as an injury.

Therefore all in the world delight to exalt him and do not weary of him. Because he does not strive, no one finds it possible to strive against him.

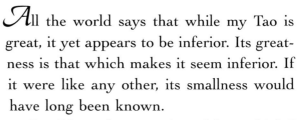

*A*ll the world says that while my Tao is great, it yet appears to be inferior. Its greatness is that which makes it seem inferior. If it were like any other, its smallness would have long been known.

But I have three precious things which I prize and hold fast. The first is gentleness; the second is frugality; the third is shrinking from seeking eminence.

With that gentleness, I can be bold; with that frugality, I can be liberal; by shrinking from seeking eminence, I can become as a vessel of the highest honor. They give up gentleness and are all for being bold; give up frugality, and are all for being liberal; give up the hindmost place, and seek only to be foremost — all of which ends in death.

Gentleness is sure to be victorious even in battle, and firmly to maintain its ground. Heaven will save its possessor, by his very gentleness protecting him.

𝓗e who has skill in wars assumes no martial stance;

He who excels in battle is not incited by anger.

He who vanquishes keeps a distance from his foes;

He whose commands men fully obey humbly plies his art.

Thus we say, "He never contends and therein lies his might."

Thus we say, "He bends men's wills so that they join him."

Thus we say, "His ends are those of Heaven, the way since the ancient sages of Heaven."

A master of the art of war has said, "I do not care to be the aggressor; I prefer to be the defender. I do not dare to advance an inch; I prefer to retire a foot."

This is called marshaling the ranks where there are no ranks; rolling up one's sleeves to fight where there are no arms to bare; grasping the weapon where there is no weapon to grasp; advancing against the enemy where there is no enemy.

There is no calamity greater than lightly engaging in war. To do that is near to losing the gentleness that is so precious. Thus it is that when the duel begins, he who deplores the situation conquers.

*M*y words are very easy to know, and very easy to practice; but there is no one in the world who is able to know and able to practice them.

In my words, there is an all-comprehending origin and an authoritative law for the things which I enforce. It is because they do not know these that men do not know me.

They who know me are few, and I am, on that account, the more to be valued. It is thus that the sage wears shabby clothes while he carries his jade in his heart.

To know and yet think we do not know is the highest; not to know and yet think that we do know is a disease.

The painful thought of this disease preserves us from it. The sage does not have the disease. He knows the pain that would be inseparable from it, and therefore he does not have it.

When the people do not fear what they ought to fear, that which is their greatest dread will come upon them.

Let them not thoughtlessly indulge themselves in their ordinary life; let them not act as if weary of what that life depends on.

It is by avoiding such indulgence that such weariness does not arise.

Therefore the sage knows of himself, but does not parade his knowledge; loves himself, but does not appear to exalt himself.

Thus he puts the latter alternative away and chooses the former.

*H*e whose boldness appears in his daring to defy law is put to death; he whose boldness appears in his not daring lives on. Of these two cases, the one appears to be advantageous, and the other to be injurious.

But when Heaven is angry, who truly knows the cause? Even the sage has difficulty.

It is the way of Heaven not to strive, and yet it skillfully overcomes; not to speak, yet it is skillful in obtaining a response; not to summon, yet men come to it on their own. Its demonstrations are quiet, yet its plans are skillful and effective.

The meshes of the net of Heaven are large and far apart, but let nothing escape.

The people do not fear death; to
what end is it to frighten them with death?

If the people were always in awe of death,
and I could always seize those who do wrong
and put them to death, who would dare to do
wrong?

There is always One who presides
over the infliction of death. He who
would inflict death in the room of the
One who presides over it may be
described as a woodcutter, not the great
carpenter. It is rare that he who under-
takes the hewing in the place of the great
carpenter does not cut his
own hands.

The people starve because of the multitude of taxes consumed by their governors. It is through this that they starve.

The people are difficult to govern because of the excessive actions of their governors. It is through this that they are difficult to govern.

The people make light of dying because of the greatness of their labors in seeking the means of living. Thus they think lightly of dying. Thus it is that it is better to leave the subject of living out entirely than to set a high value on it.

*A*t his birth man is supple and weak; at his death he is firm and strong. So it is with all things. Trees and plants, in their early growth, are soft and tender; at their death, they are dry and withered.

Thus it is that firmness and strength are the concomitants of death; softness and weakness the concomitants of life.

Hence he who relies on the strength of his forces does not conquer, and a tree which is strong will fill outstretched arms and invites the axe.

Therefore the place of what is firm and strong falls below, and that of the soft and the weak rises above.

May not the Way of Heaven be compared to the bending of a bow? The part of the bow which was high is brought low, and what was low is raised up. So Heaven diminishes where there is superabundance and supplements where there is deficiency.

It is the Way of Heaven to diminish superabundance, and to supplement deficiency. It is not so with the way of man. He takes away from those who do not have enough to add to his own superabundance.

Who can take his own superabundance and therewith serve all under heaven? Only he who possesses the Tao!

Therefore the sage acts without claiming the results as his; he achieves his merit and does not rest in it; he does not wish to display his superiority.

There is nothing in the world more soft and weak than water, and yet for attacking things that are firm and strong, nothing can surpass it. Nothing can take its place.

Everyone in the world knows that the soft overcomes the hard, and the weak the strong, but no one is able to carry it out in practice.

Therefore a sage has said, "He who takes on the state's reproach is the lord of its altars; he who takes on all men's woes is a worthy king."

Words that are strictly true seem paradoxical.

When two reconcile after great animosity, there is sure to be a grudge in the mind of the one who was wrong. How does this benefit the other?

Therefore the sage keeps the left-hand portion of the contract, and does not insist on the fulfillment of it by the other party. He who is virtuous regards only the conditions of the engagement, while he who lacks virtue regards only the conditions favorable to himself.

In the Way of Heaven, there is no partiality of love; it is always on the side of the good man.

In a little state with a small population, though there be individuals with the abilities of ten or a hundred men, there should be no employment of them; I would make the people, while looking on death as a grievous thing, not move elsewhere to avoid it.

Though they had boats and carriages, they should have no occasion to ride in them; though they had armor and sharp weapons, they should have no occasion to wear or use them.

I would make the people return to the use of knotted cords instead of written characters.

They should think their plain foods sweet; their coarse clothes beautiful; their poor dwellings places of rest; and their common and simple ways sources of enjoyment.

Though there be a neighboring state within sight, and the crowing of the roosters and the barking of the dogs be heard from one place to another, I would make the people, to old age and even to death, have no communication with it.

Sincere words are not fine; fine words are not sincere. Those who are skilled do not dispute; the disputatious are not skilled in it. Those who know are not extensively learned; the extensively learned do not know it.

The sage does not accumulate. The more he expends for others, the more does he possess of his own; the more that he gives to others, the more does he have himself.

With all the sharpness of the Way of Heaven, it does not injure; with all the doing in the way of the sage, he does not strive.